VACATION RENTAL REVOLUTION

James McCullough

Copyright © 2020 James McCullough

All rights reserved

The characters and events portrayed in this book are fictitious. Any similarity to real persons, living or dead, is coincidental and not intended by the author.

No part of this book may be reproduced, or stored in a retrieval system, or transmitted in any form or by any means, electronic, mechanical, photocopying, recording, or otherwise, without express written permission of the publisher.

ISBN-13: 9798619218534

Printed in the United States of America

CONTENTS

Title Page
Copyright
Epigraph
Introduction
Prepare   1
Research   4
Space   11
Price   15
Expenses   19
Marketing   24
Launch   34
Appendix   36
Contact   38
About The Author   39

An essential intent is both inspirational and concrete, both meaningful and measurable. Done right, an essential intent is one decision that settles one thousand later decisions. It's like deciding you're going to become a doctor instead of a lawyer. One strategic choice eliminates a universe of other options and maps a course for the next five, ten, or even twenty years of your life. Once the big decision is made, all subsequent decisions come into better focus.

GREG MCKEOWN

INTRODUCTION

The hunt is on for individual experiences, a story that can be shared with their friends and family. People are seeking out two different types of places to stay: boutique hotels and vacation homes.

There is a global trend happening that is scaring many in the hospitality industry: people are starting to stay away from the large hotels and wanting a more personable stay. The hunt is on for individual experiences, a story that can be shared with their friends and family. That drive to find that story is starting in two different types of accommodations: boutique hotels and vacation homes. The latter allows for the most personable experience and is exploding in popularity.

It is a hospitality revolution. A great shift in booking trends that is being experienced around the world, all at the same time. People are booking spaces of all sizes and varieties: condos, whole homes, a bedroom, a houseboat, and villas able to accommodate 40 people. You can find these spaces in all corners of the world, from the Klondike Gold Rush town of Dawson City, Yukon, the remote Easter Island, to Kigali, Rwanda. The best part is there is always space for more homes and properties to jump in to be a part of the global trend, not to be excluding from it.

Creating that experience for these travelers is just as rewarding for the owners of the vacation rental. Meeting people from other parts of the world, sharing stories about your individual journeys, and, sharing the city you live in with others can bring a great joy within you that can't be found elsewhere. One of the most rewarding experiences is telling someone a place you enjoy eating at or visiting, and then having them repeat their positive experience back to you. A journey created by both parties that starts at your own home.

Not only is operating a vacation rental rewarding for your personal enjoyment, it can be financially lucrative. Depending on how large of a space you are willing to share with others, it can pay for your monthly expenses, your monthly mortgage payments, or become a major source of income. With the global trend moving to these smaller spaces, the potential to earn income with a rental property is going to exist for a long time yet. That is a great positive for anyone looking to explore the possibility of operating your own rental property.

There are seven steps that lead towards joining this revolution. The purpose of this small book is to lead you through those steps, giving you some ideas on what to expect, what to prepare for, and to help you decide whether to make the leap to join in. It is not the ultimate guide in how to operate your property. With the variety of properties available to stay in, there are equally as many ways to operate them. The ultimate decision comes down to personal choice and comfort levels.

This book is to help you discover your comfort levels when it involves your property and lead you to make the best choices possible. So, grab a notepad and pen to make some notes, a cup of coffee or tea, and prepare to learn all about the ongoing vacation property revolution.

PREPARE

Making the decision to share your personal space with strangers is not an easy one to make. There will always be doubts in your mind of whether you can trust the other party to pay you on time and not damage the belongings. There will be constant questioning of whether you will have guests to stay in your place, as well. The growing unease a vacation property owner feels is shared equally with the party booking with them though.

Making the choice to book with an owner directly is a big risk. It is not always as secure as booking with a hotel in several different ways. First of all, there is no guarantee that you will even have a place to stay in. There are major scams happening on other advertising sites (namely Craigslist). People duplicate listings found on the main booking sites, like AirBnB and HomeAway, collect deposits from people, and then the people show up expecting to have a place to stay. The owners are dumbfounded because they had no idea their listing had been duplicated, and the people are furious because they have lost their money to some stranger. It is not an easy position to be in for either party.

The second major risk is that the place they have booked may not be the place they end up staying. People fake their images all the time or show a well-kept place, only to not maintain that cleanliness or have the same furniture. It is certainly upsetting to book a place expecting a pool, only to find out that the pool is not maintained, or worse, non-existent.

Neither problem generally happens with hotels, because you can confirm all the details in advance. There will be reviews to read on TripAdvisor, pictures on the internet to confirm the room layouts and location of the hotels, and better safety measures in place with your credit card company to protect you from fraudulent use. If the room is not as maintained as you expected, you switch hotels, and escape any charges from the hotel.

The risk factor is being mentioned at the beginning, because it is something you cannot escape after making the decision to book your place. There are other ways that can prevent you from having a rewarding experience that will be discussed later on, but the trust issue is front and center. It is something that will be questioned constantly as people confirm their bookings with you, question payments and refunds, and want to make direct contact with you on the phone in advance. You have to be comfortable with accepting these risks, and also be comfortable in reassuring others that you can be trusted in ensuring everything will be fine.

This reassurance becomes easier the more you practice it, and the questioning becomes less annoying than they are at first. And they will be annoying. It will likely be one of the few times in your life where there is doubt being shown towards who you are, where you live, and whether you are a good person or not.

Now that the risk factor has been discussed, we can move along on this journey.

TYPES OF RENTALS

As mentioned before, people are seeking out and staying at a variety of different places. Apart from the general condo and house, you can choose to stay at a farmhouse, at a castle, on a yacht or houseboat, or in a mill. Visit Granada, Spain, and you have your choice of houses to stay in that are located in caves. The variety to be found is astounding. There are hidden gems everywhere you look in the world, too. Everyone is offering a new and unique experience to be discovered.

The types of spaces available is not the only difference that can occur. There can be different experiences involved when checking into a place: do you collect the key from a lockbox located outside, greeted by a doorman, or is the owner actually staying within the home with you? Some people seek out the human experience, others avoid it.

You may not own a house in a cave, but the main take-away is to start thinking about the experience you can offer in your place. From the location of the rental and activities in the immediate area, to the amenities found within your place. The more individualized your place is, the greater it will stand out as people search online for a place to stay.

The next decision to make is how much space you want to share with others. There are budget travelers who are seeking out only a bedroom, crashing on a couch, or there are professionals and families seeking out whole units. If you are venturing into this with hesitation, perhaps you will feel more comfortable having a listing for only a bedroom or two and operate as a small bed and breakfast. If are you more dedicated to the idea and have another space to stay, creating a full listing for the entire house or condo may be the smart decision to make.

With all of this in mind, the potential risks and how much space you are willing to share, we can venture forth into the nitty gritty of setting up the details of your vacation rental through some careful research.

RESEARCH

One of the most important steps in deciding whether to commit to having a vacation rental is doing the research to make an informed decision. This research can be incredibly detailed like a large hotel would do in creating a business plan, or it can be a simplified version. The simpler version of the business plan will suffice for a single unit rental and the elements to it will be laid out below. They will guide you in developing a more thorough plan to help ease your mind a bit through this whole process.

There are three main areas we need to look at with our research:
1. How many listings are available for your neighbourhood, and city?
2. How many hotels will you be competing with?
3. How is the tourism and rental market doing for your city?

Within each area, there are two areas of focus: the size of the market, and also information about pricing. These will guide a lot of decisions that will be made through this entire process, especially when it comes to marketing and pricing.

Before that happens though, we need to look at local regulations surrounding vacation rentals. Many cities are becoming more restrictive about short-term rental properties, because of the loss of revenue through hotel taxes. The hotel taxes generally pay for the marketing of the city/region nationally or internationally, plus help pay for visitor information centers. The threat of losing that revenue has seen many cities enact bylaws to force these short-term rentals into paying the same hotel tax, registering as a business, and paying separate business dues. It is definitely something to look into before starting or risk some consequences.

The other regulations to be aware of are more specific to people living in condos that have strata regulations. Some strata corporations are severely restrictive in how many rentals are allowed in the building, and for a set duration. Others have unlimited numbers of rentals, but restrict them to be annual terms. There are complexes out there that are designed for short-term rentals, though, and may even have a rental pool office to help manage your rental. Going against the strata corporation can cause major problems. The corporation can take you to court to collect fines, and in some extreme cases, even force you to sell your unit. Caution before proceeding and a full investigation into strata bylaws is strongly encouraged.

Once that decision has been made for you about the legalities surrounding a short-term rental, then we can move on and complete the research.

NEIGHBOURHOOD AND CITY

Depending on how large your neighbourhood and city is, this area of research may take up a good chunk of time. You need to investigate the size of the market you are entering, paying close attention to units that are similar to yours. You need to be aware of the variety of units available to rent and how many of your own type are available.

By type, I mean as many specifics as you can define: number of bedrooms and bathrooms, special amenities like pools, fireplaces, hot tubs, access to special facilities for fitness or tennis, and privacy, private balconies or tree-lined backyards. Anything you would be looking for when purchasing a house or condo, is exactly what people are looking for when seeking out their own vacation home. Remember, these people are looking to not book at a hotel that has shared facilities and very limited with privacy.

The good thing is the main booking portals, AirBnB and HomeAway, come with filters that allow you to narrow down your search results to match the unit you are going to be renting out. I create a spreadsheet to keep track of what I find, listing the neighbourhood, number of units similar to mine, and number of units overall. I also tend to keep a separate spreadsheet to keep a tally on the pricing, which will be discussed in a later chapter.

One factor that will help you decide whether to enter a market or not will be how saturated it is. If you live in downtown of a major city or you are close to a major attraction like a beach, there is likely always going to be room for more. If you live in a small village and there are already ten listings, it may not be a great idea to start up a new rental property. It all depends on how different your property is compared to the competition.

The other important factor is availability. In that small village with ten listings, is there demand for more or not? The best way to find out the answer to that question is by searching the peak season dates and paying attention to the number of listings that get displayed. Generally speaking, if you are looking at a major holiday weekend, you should see fewer listings be displayed than if you left the dates open-ended. That will be a great indicator in how likely your unit will be booked up in your high season. If the number of listings drops to a low percentage being available, demand is high; if the high number barely drops, demand is low and not a good market to enter into.

The trump card in all this is what you have to offer and its location. If the majority of the vacation units are far from your unit, there may be an opportunity to enter the market. This is especially true if you are close to a major tourist attraction. Having a draw to your area will only help you in securing future bookings. Likewise, if your place compares extremely well to the others, there will also be the opportunity to enter the market. If the others do not have any amenities, or perhaps your place can accommodate a lot more people, the revenue potential will be there for you.

HOTELS

Your main competition will be other vacation rentals, since that is what people are searching for, but hotels are just as important. They provide a good baseline for what dollar amount you can expect from your space. Hotel rooms will likely be smaller than what you will be offering, but their amenities may be more enhanced than yours: fitness centers, spa facilities, in-hotel coffee shops, and so forth.

Keeping a tab on the hotel industry will help you in your pursuits while renting out the vacation rental. The most obvious reason is, "Where will people stay when all the hotels are sold out?" The likely answer will be in vacation rentals, if they are available in the city.

The other reason to keep an eye on them is to be aware of where they are advertising. Hotels generally do not have the marketing funds to blanket the market with advertising. They have to remain focused to attract the right type of guest to stay at their hotel. The guests that are spending the money to travel, and the guests who will take advantage of their services and appreciate them the most. It makes little sense for a luxury hotel with spa facilities to be advertising on University campuses. The guests who would be staying at that hotel are not going to be on campus or be too few to make it worthwhile to spend the money in pursuit of them. The areas where hotels are advertising are likely the best areas to be looking for your guests.

It is also important to be aware of any deals that may pop up in their advertising with specific dates being mentioned. Hotel promotions are targeted like their advertising is: promoting the time period where the occupancy has been historically lower compared to other periods. It is quite rare to find a promotion being run for the peak dates of a summer season when the city is going to be full regardless of the hotel rates. Just because a hotel is offering a promotion and dropping their rates, does not necessarily mean your property should drop its rates, as well. Hotels have many more opportunities to have additional costs once the guest is at the hotel in order to make up for lost revenue. More expensive items in a minibar, a price bump for wireless internet access, limited offerings in the restaurant, and so forth. Promotions can be quite deceiving in that the hotel room rate is not always the most important to the hotel.

Like using AirBnB or HomeAway to track vacation rentals, it is easiest to use a site like Booking.com to find all the hotels available in your area with their going rates. Rates are usually synchronized with the hotel's system to ensure a rate parity across all their various booking channels. Because of this, it saves a lot of time when doing research to look at Booking.com, instead of browsing all the individual hotel sites. You will be able to see all the hotel rates, their locations, and different hotel room types being offered. Booking.com also lets you filter down into different rental properties, like vacation rentals, instead of large hotels.

Expedia should be avoiding when completing research, partly because almost all hotels have listings on Booking.com now, and because they take nearly double the commission that Booking.com does, which allows them more flexibility with rate adjustments. If they choose to lower the hotel rate by $20, they are not affecting the net revenues earned by the hotel, only the amount of their own commission. Expedia helps control the hotel market in this way be creating a false sense of demand in the market. Discount an unpopular hotel, fill up their allotment of hotel rooms to Expedia, and then book the hotels with higher rates where Expedia can make up ground with its commission structure.

Apart from pricing, Booking.com allows you to get a sense of the availability for hotel rooms in the market. After entering a search for a specific date, a banner appears at the top of the listings to announce the availability of the city on those dates. It will also mention in the search results whether a particular is sold out instead of eliminating it from the list. Valuable information if you want to gauge demand for a period of time in the city surrounding popular events.

TOURISM AND RENTAL MARKET

The majority of large cities, and even small cities, will have a tourism organization in control of the visitor information centers and marketing the city/area to a larger public. They are either affiliated with a local or municipal government, which requires them to track and release information to help guide city or regional planning. They will generally release annual reports to their members and the larger business community to assist them with their own planning, as well, which means the reports are accessible to the public.

These reports can be very specific about where people are traveling from, and how they are reaching the area. If the city or region is close to a border crossing, they will likely also contain that information, mentioning which border crossings are busier than the others. The border information may not appear to be very useful, but it will help guide potential marketing strategies if you have a marketing campaign for a larger number of units to rent.

Where people are coming from and how many people are traveling are the main metrics to be aware of. The reports will include trends to show growth patterns or drops in traffic, which will help you make the decision to enter the rental market or not. They should also help confirm which months are busiest for tourism activities in the region, which will influence pricing strategies and when you want to have your property available for short-term rentals.

The rental market will be reported on by various organizations, from municipal and territorial governments to help with their planning, or in the media to help notify the larger business and developer communities. The reports should be accessible by contacting the local governments to enquire about the report, or a quick search on Google will help you find the appropriate news media articles. In Canada, this information is controlled by the Canada Mortgage and Housing Corporation for cities with more than 10,000 people. In the United States, data is collected by Reis Inc.

The report will generally state a number for the total rentable units, a vacancy rate for them, and an average rent cost for various sized units. The information will tell you how the market is increasing or shrinking with total units available, and also how much demand there tends to be. This is valuable for the off-season of your vacation rental. For example, the units in my complex are mainly rented out on a short-term basis from May until the end of August. For September until the end of April, the units are almost always rented out to University students on a 8 month lease. Demand in the city is extremely high, which allows the owners of these units to charge a premium and cover their monthly costs, while making the majority of their money in the busy summer season here.

Between all three areas of research, you should be able to gather more than enough information to help guide you through the rest of the planning process for your vacation rental.

SPACE

Defining space is something most people enjoy doing in their own homes. Always on the lookout for the perfect item to enhance the interior decoration of the home, or a furniture piece with more function, a better bed, and so forth. Most people enjoy re-arranging furniture to suit their purposes as their needs change over time. With a vacation rental, the moments to define the space are more limited, because you have to work around your guests staying there.

It will be important to plan and define the space you are renting out with other people in mind, not just how you would enjoy being in it. What may be appealing to you, may not be to them. A comfortable chair that conforms to your body likely will not match up well with others. The best way to approach this is to design a space that will be aesthetically pleasing to attract as many people as possible, and also be flexible enough to allow the occupants to adjust the space to fit their needs.

The other important element to keep in mind is that you cannot control your occupants in how they treat your furnishings. Things may get damaged, small items may become lost, and there is potential for fabrics to be stained. Not only will you have to design a space that is flexible for your guests, but you will also have to have a place that can be easily replaced if need be. As much as you enjoy that one-of-a-kind painting done for you personally by that street artist in Paris, are you comfortable with it being in your rental and being ruined for good?

There are many ways to handle both designing a flexible and replaceable space. The flexible part will be of personal taste. It should include light weight end tables or coffee tables, upright lamps, or chairs that can be easily moved by one person, or blinds that are easy to use to control light. Hotel rooms are generally fairly static in their placement of furniture, because there is hardly any room to move around or the furniture is too heavy to be moved easily. With vacation rentals, the opposite should be true. The guests will be in there multiple nights, perhaps even multiple weeks, and will want to make the space as comfortable as they can with how they like to live. The most extreme example I have personally experienced is a couple who had to bring not only their own pillows, but also their own Keurig coffee machine so they were guaranteed to have the coffee they liked best each morning. I have also had people bring their own plants to have in the unit because they were going to be there for several weeks.

Those are both outliers, but it's important to keep in mind that the space is for them, not you, when renting it out.

When furnishing the vacation rental, it may be best to stick to furniture from one or two stores. If something is damaged, they will likely have something in a similar style that you can put in its place, or even buy the same item again. It helps keep a cohesive look to the space, as well. When picking out the store to buy the furniture in, I would suggest avoiding cheap materials and constructions. You want the furniture to last and it will get banged up easily, even if you think otherwise. Buying the cheap furniture means replacing it more often, which adds in more hassles for you to deal with- ordering, picking up, and installing. It can be a better investment to choose something more expensive, so it lasts longer, but not something beyond your budget that is not easily replaced.

Apart from furnishings, there are a few other key things to consider when planning your vacation rental. Sheets and linens are going to be washed frequently and may get stained from makeup. There is a reason why hotels mainly purchase white towels and linens: easy to clean. A lot of stores now sell sheet sets and towels that are heavier-duty and may even mention on the labelling that they are meant for hotels. These sets will handle the washing and drying cycles much better than regular sheets. You may be washing them every other night, depending on how long your guests stay, so it will save you some money in the long run.

The other thing to consider will be all your amenities that will be included in the vacation rental. This includes a wide assortment of items, from the television and stereo system, the kitchen utensils, to plates and dishes. Like the furniture, it will be important to plan ahead for items breaking accidentally. Dishes and glassware will be more easily replaceable, but it is suggested you buy extras and store them off-site from the vacation rental so they are ready to go when needed. For the kitchen accessories, the longer you think guests will be staying in your place, the better equipped to be. A full list of items to consider will be in the appendix, but it includes items you may not initially think about, like storage containers, a blender, and dish towels.

Beyond the kitchen, items to consider will include cleaning supplies for quick spills, iron and ironing board, spare Kleenex boxes, a portable speaker with a dock for an iPod/iPhone, extra coat hangers, shampoo, conditioner, body soaps, and makeup remover.

After all those items are considered, you can think more about how you want to personalize the experience for your guests. Do you want to have a library of classic books to read, or various coffee table photo-books? Do you want to invest in an Google Chromecast or Amazon Fire Stick to offer Netflix easily on the TV? Do you have space for a BBQ on your balcony or deck? If you do, don't forget all the utensils that will be needed. There are many more ways in how you can add a bit of flavour to your space. The more visual aids will stand out when people are browsing the listings looking at pictures, the physical amenities will stand out for when people are searching for the listings. Anything that will give you a slight edge and help encourage people to stay with you will be a bonus.

When you are making decisions for all the amenities and furnishings, make a mental note in your head about who you are designing the space for. Who will be staying there the majority of the time and what will help attract others to stay there? The more amenities you can include that are within your budget, the more likely you will be able to boost your prices up, as well. A lot of things to consider when planning your space, but they are very important things to decide on before moving on to the next step.

PRICE

Price is likely the trickiest part to get right when preparing to have a vacation rental available. There is no magic formula to get it right the first time and can be seen more as an art than a science to get it right. It all comes down to does it feel right to you, and does it feel valuable for your guest?

The whole process for deciding on a rate is based on all the research that was completed earlier: your competition with other vacation rentals, hotels, and also how well the overall market is faring. It will be easiest to look over it all if you take the time to enter it into a spreadsheet, which helps with organizing the data, but also lets you do quick calculations without punching in many numbers into a calculator. Group the competition numbers by how similar they are to you, then the closest competition that offers more than you (i.e. if you are offering a two bedroom condo, look at the three bedroom condos or a two bedroom house), and finally the competition that offers less than you (i.e. a one bedroom condo.) For all three areas, I would include any hotels that match that category, or have a fourth group of hotel rooms that closely match what you are offering. I would not be too concerned about hotel rooms that are much better or worse than what you are offering, as they aren't really your competition.

The first step in the process is to define the times you will be operating, and then divide that timeframe into smaller chunks, called a season. For some people, they could have a year-round rental. For others, they have short-term rentals through the high season, and then longer-term through the off-season (off referring to not as busy or desirable compared to the high season.) A lot of this decision will be decided upon how valuable you believe your rental is and how likely it will be rented during the slower off-season. For example, a condo located downtown in a city will likely be rented out year-round, but a chalet on a ski hill will most likely not be as desirable during the off-season when there is no snow on the ground and services available.

To help you in making this decision, look at what your main competition is doing. If you have other units available near you when the traffic is going to be smaller, there is likely enough demand there for you to enter the market. You can check to see how many units are available by doing searches for broad periods of time a year or two in advance when fewer people have booked. A quick note about each period will show you the pattern of how many units are available. As an example, in my home city of Kelowna, BC, there are approximately 230 units available in the summer season. In the winter season, it drops down to 150 units. If I were to apply more filters to align with my actual property, the numbers go from 114 in summertime to 60 in the off-season. That's quite a large drop-off, which is why I only rent out during the busy summer season and then have students occupy the unit from September to April so I'm not left with an empty unit.

As mentioned before, you can break down your year into seasons. The seasons will be based on the times you can expect to receive the most occupants, which will vary from region to region and what kind of unit you are renting out. Here are three examples of how a year could be broken down for my city. Three different units in different locations:

- May-late June
- Late June-late August
- September-April

- April-late June
- Late June-late August

- September-late October
- November-March

- Spring Break
- Spring Break-Snow Melt
- May-October
- November-Christmas Break
- Christmas Break
- Christmas Break-Spring Break

Within those seasons, you can break things down further: long weekends or special events (like a county fair, music festival, sports competition) could be priced slightly higher than the usual rate, Once the seasons are defined, we can go to the spreadsheet and see how the rates look when being compared in a narrow fashion. Take the average rate for your first competitive group, and then the average for the lower third of the units in the second competitive group. The range of rates will be the benchmark for where to place your own unit's prices.

For a first-year operation that is feeling slightly hesitant about entering the market, I would price on the lower end of the scale and look at pricing again for the following season. If you sold out easily, then you can move your prices up higher and make-up for the losses encountered in the first season. If you are more financially secure in case the unit doesn't rent out as much as expected, you can do the opposite and scale to the higher-end the first season, then drop down for the second if need be.

Enter your rates into a final spreadsheet to keep track of so you can enter them on the booking sites on a consistent basis, your website, and can provide accurate quotes if taking manual bookings. It will also help you when looking back over previous years to see what rate you charged a few years ago and how it compares to now. For people with multiple units of the same variety, one strategy to use is to scale one unit higher than the other and see how it books in comparison.

Through this whole process of setting rates, it is important to remain flexible and not become married to the rates you are setting. If you are a month away from your busy season and you are not receiving as many bookings as you thought, you can drop your rates down a notch to capture as many reservations as you can. This should not be a problem if you follow the pricing guidelines mentioned above.

EXPENSES

After talking about pricing, the natural thing to do is to calculate the revenue potential for the vacation rental. You likely worked out a nice, surprising number after working out the total cost someone will spend for staying a week, multiplied how many weeks there are in your seasons. That number is nice, but one cannot forget that there will be expenses involved in attaining that amount.

The expenses involved in operating a vacation will scale up depending on how large the unit is and should be on a slow decline the longer your rental is available over-time. The costs scale upwards because of the additional cleaning costs, more energy to cool or heat the unit, and more likely more laundry that needs to be done. Costs should decline overtime as you have more return guests and have a better idea of marketing costs (eliminating some methods or subscribing to more financially beneficial plans.)

Below will be more discussion about the areas that fluctuate from guest to guest or can be more easily controlled. When working out the net income for a unit, it will be important to include some other costs that will be fixed on a monthly basis: mortgage payments, strata/maintenance fees, cable/WiFi costs, electricity, and gas costs. I would also suggest spreading your property taxes equally over the full calendar year or the period where you generate the bulk of your income.

There are several areas of a vacation rental to keep it running smoothly:

- Management (reservations and marketing)
- Cleaning/Maintenance (cleaning, laundry, replacing amenities)

MANAGEMENT COSTS

The management role involves setting up all the marketing, handling the bookings, taking in the deposits, and coordinating with the person in charge of cleaning. Some of the tasks could be delegated to someone else, while the owners handle the rest, or a property manager handles it all while the owners remain hands off. Of course, the owners may wish to be fully involved and operate everything on their own to cut down on extra expenses. If you are planning to go that route, you may wish to skip ahead to the discussion of cleaning costs.

Depending on what kind of role a property manager will have, their fees will vary, and it may will also depend on your region. For where I am in British Columbia, Canada, property managers have to be licensed and be associated with a real estate brokerage. It provides security in how they operate, but also means that the costs are going to be slightly higher than if they were unlicensed and did not offer the additional security.

Generally, property managers will work on a fee-based contract, not hourly, because reservations can occur at any time and there may be times where they are waiting on a guest to depart to get it ready for the next person. Some property management companies may also work on a commission-based fee, especially if they have full control over setting the rates and marketing on top of their usual tasks. This commission structure will vary depending on the potential revenues being brought in, but a good rule of thumb is the fee will be between 30-50% of the revenues. If the property manager is responsible for finding the cleaning company to use, that cost may be included in their fee. In general, the cleaning costs will be on top of the property manager. Something to keep in mind when deciding how you want to operate.

A property manager can be quite valuable in helping setup your full marketing plan, providing a pricing strategy, and consulting with you about what amenities to include in your unit. As when hiring anyone, it is suggested that you ask for some referrals from the property manager or management company to ensure that they have a track record of being successful with rentals in the past. It will offer you some protection before hiring someone who ends up renting your unit for less than market value or to less desirable guests.

There are other expenses attached to the reservations and marketing, which will be handled in the next chapter.

CLEANING AND MAINTENANCE COSTS

The cleaning and maintaining of the vacation rental will be the most time consuming and laborious act once the rental is open for business. Depending on the size of your unit and the amount of free time you have, it may be better to hire someone or a company to handle the cleaning needs. Included with the cleaning of the unit will be washing all the linens and towels, which is time-consuming in itself.

The costs of a cleaning company will vary greatly depending on where the unit is located, because of different minimum wage rules. Companies will charge above minimum wage to handle the additional costs involved, which should also include cleaning supplies. If you choose to supply your own cleaning supplies, the cost should be lower, but you may encounter companies that are reluctant to use different materials than what they provide. Mainly so they can protect the health of their employees, but also so they can guarantee the cleanliness of the unit. The last thing cleaning companies want to deal with is inferior products or a lack of supply when they show up to complete a job.
Because of the variations in the cost of a cleaning company, it can be difficult to give you a rough estimate of the costs to be ex-

pected. There are some general rules you can apply to work out the total time involved in cleaning the unit though. The larger the space, the longer it will take, is obvious, but we also need to factor in kitchen, how many bathrooms and bedrooms, and outdoor space. To estimate the time involved, here are some suggestions on time needed to clean:

Living Space x 30 mins per 500 sq ft
Number of Bathrooms x 20 mins
Number of Bedrooms x 20 mins
Kitchen x 30 mins
Number of Patio Spaces x 15 mins

For the kitchen, I would increase the time involved if there are multiple ovens, larger counters for an island, and if there are any extra appliances. If the dishwasher cycle is less than the total cleaning time estimate, make sure to include that in.

It will also be important to factor in time involved with washing and drying towels and linens if that is to be done on site, instead of handling it at your house or other facility. I suggest handling the laundry off-site and having an extra set of everything brought over with the cleaning company. This allows the cleaners to do their job without having to wait for the sheets or towels to finish drying. Any time spent waiting while in the unit is going to be charged to you so it is important to be fully prepared for their arrival.

Calculating the cleaning time in advance will be extremely useful for you because it will be an important factor in when you take reservations. If you have a checkout time of 11:00 AM, and it takes four hours for the cleaning of the unit, then you can't have a guaranteed check-in time of 2:00 PM. Of course, if you have a much larger space (backyard with a pool, for example), you may require a full day of preparation which will have to be factored in for how you market your place.

On top of cleaning time, you will also have to be aware of the additional costs involved in stocking up bathrooms, the kitchen, and living space. Refillable bottles for shampoo and conditioner, new bars of soap laid out with every stay, dishwasher capsules or soap, Kleenex, laundry detergent, and, of course, toilet paper. Everything will be used much quicker than you first realize. It will be a good idea to have a small batch of extras on-site in case people run through the full supply, but not enough to invite temptation in taking things (which happens.) To keep fully stock of these supplies, places like Costco will be your best friend in helping keep your maintenance costs to a minimum.

MARKETING

Spreading the word that you have a vacation rental available is the most important area of a first-year operation. The best way to discover something new, whether it is music or a place to travel to, is by word of mouth. In the first year of operation, word of mouth is not something you can rely on because no one has stayed at your place as a vacation rental yet. The key is to get your first guests and then things will become easier as they tell more people, people see reviews of your unit online, and your rank on the various sites rises due to your bookings.

The best way to think of marketing is that it acts like a funnel to direct people to the end destination of your place. That destination is going to be your starting point in building outwards, which will be the first choice you make in setting up the vacation rental. A website is a common destination but can cost additional money. A Facebook page is free, but not as professional looking as a separate webpage. Or you could use the listing address of your vacation rental on a site like AirBnB or HomeAway/VRBO. Ultimately, you will most likely be setting up the profiles on the rental sites, and Facebook since it is free, so the decision boils down to whether you want a full-blown website or not. Let's start the discussion there.

WEBSITE AND CHANNEL MANAGER

There are basically three different options for a website for a vacation rental:

      1. A full website which allows people to make bookings

via an email form
2. A simple landing page which is a jumping off point for your listings on different sites
3. A website that is integrated with a channel manager that allows for online bookings

A full website can be expensive if you are looking to offer a professional experience without any clunky web addresses (i.e. myrental.wix.com) or corporate branding. It can also be a bit overkill, because you will likely not have enough information to build a full website. You will want a page with your images, contact information and how to make a booking, and information about the rental (rates, location, any special rules.) The other things to consider would be things to do in the city/region with links to other resources. Because the information is much simpler for vacation rentals, I would suggest scaling down to only a landing page.

Landing pages are becoming more common now when dealing with one main focus. Examples would include selling a book, an online course, announcing a new app for an iPhone, and so forth. They look great because they are usually one scrolling page, no advertising, and no clunky interface. They are just as flexible as a full webpage though, including different widgets to show a gallery of pictures, pull information in from social media, and more.

Wordpress.com is my preferred place to go, because there is a lot of additional support for them with different themes. You can build a free site to get started with the ability to add different functionality to the site. The editor is quite easy to use and all your changes are viewed in real-time, meaning no coding required. Even better, you can purchase a theme that can be easily modified for a vacation rental. The booking links would direct to your listing on either AirBnB, HomeAway, or other booking service you would like to use.

A channel manager is the next step up which ties together a website with the ability to take reservations online directly from your site. They include a credit card processor to accept deposits or full payments, ways to manage your bookings (change dates, cancel), and also what they call a channel manager, the ability to bring in all the reservation details from AirBnB, HomeAway, and other sites so all the information is in one place. That way, if someone makes a booking on AirBnB, it will prevent people from making the reservation on HomeAway, and vice versa. If you are going to branch out your listing to multiple sites, it will be much easier to manage if using a channel manager to control everything.

There are plenty of channel managers on the market, most will have free trials to let you see how it functions, but the monthly costs will be affordable. Because it functions as a website, too, you won't need to setup a paid landing page or website through a different service. There are a list of various channel managers in the Appendix, but my preferred one is Lodgify. The layout of their webpages is beautiful, and there is full flexibility in how to design it- adjust the colours as needed, various layouts, include other elements on the page as you see fit. The channel manager has worked seamlessly for me, as well, with no issues. I definitely suggest taking a look at it.

AIRBNB, HOMEWAY, AND OTHERS

Booking portals for rentals are popping up everywhere and are becoming a dime a dozen. Each site appears to have a different marketing strategy in where the listings are located in the world, so I suggest doing a bit of research to see which site has the most listings for your area.
There are a few exceptions, which are the big ones you have likely heard of: AirBnB, HomeAway, and a new one from Booking.com,

Villas.com.

When operating a vacation rental, it is highly recommended you have a listing on each one to maximize your marketing efforts in getting the word out about your listing. Basic listings are free on all three, but they differ in how they handle commissions or fees. Below is a table to demonstrate the differences in their costs. Besides the cost structures, the listings and services are essentially the same: you include images, description, rules for the unit, and can modify your prices based on seasons. Plus having the ability to close off the listing as needed to prevent overbooking your space.

RENTAL SITE	HOST FEES	GUEST FEES
AirBnB	3% per booking	6% to 12% fee depending on property.
HomeAway/VRBO	$349 to $999 annual subscription OR 10% to 13% per booking	No guest fees.
Villas.com	15% commission	No guest fees.

For the first year, I would suggest taking advantage of the free options for the services and discover the mix of where your bookings are coming from. AirBnB is generally good about promoting the new listings when they become live to help the owners in generating some initial income. There is no option to pay to boost your listing, which means you have to rely on the reviews being left by previous renters to help raise your listing in the search results. Eventually, you become a Super Host and will be even higher than the others. It will take time, but you can achieve great success through AirBnB.

HomeAway promotes its listings based on their subscriber plan, meaning the more you spend advertising your site, the higher it appears in the search results. The positive about subscribing to HomeAway is they eliminate the processing fees usually associated with the reservations. Plans start at $349.00 for the year, which means you need to generate revenues of at least $3,500.00 to make it worthwhile and save on the commission fees. The first year of operation, I hovered right at the break-even point. In the second year of operation, the revenues were much higher. If I had not been on a subscriber plan, I would have lost $500+ to the commissions. A rather significant percentage of the overall revenues.

Villas.com is fairly new, but a great opportunity for vacation rentals. It is owned and operated by Booking.com, which means all the listings on Villas.com will be appearing on the Booking.com site when searches are done. Booking.com has been showing vacation rentals for several years now. Having a separate site for vacation rentals will be a major boost for the listings. As for commissions, they will be charging 15% commission on all revenues, with no fees for the guests. Information about how they promote listings will come out in time as the service grows and more experimentation happens. It is free to build a listing and well worth exploring in the meantime.

Regardless of where you list your vacation rental, you will need to build a profile that lets your unit shine. Aim to get at least ten pictures of your unit and the immediate surrounding area to help your potential guests decide to stay there. If there are common areas that the guests can enjoy, be sure to include pictures of those areas too, as pictures speak much louder than words. Have professional pictures done if you are concerned about photo quality using a photographer recommended by a local real estate office. They will be able to capture the unit perfectly.

With the listing details, you want to be as thorough as you possibly can. Listings don't need to be very wordy as people will make their decisions based on location, amenities, and price. I would suggest putting as much emphasis on what is around your unit as what is in it, as most people will be out exploring the area more than they will be staying indoors. Double check all information before publishing the listing too. The worst thing to happen would be publishing details like the wrong check-in or out time, or not telling people that your unit is non-smoking. As long as all the information is current and easy to understand, guests will have everything they need to make the right choice.

SOCIAL MEDIA

After setting up your destination page and your listings on the various portal sites, the next step is trying to assist in driving traffic to your main destination page. Social media is all the rage right now, but when it comes to the hospitality industry, people are torn about how useful it actually is in driving traffic to a hotel or rental. Social media is useful in helping people make a decision in the moment: donate to a charity, buy a book, show support for some other cause, or make arrangements on a place to dine at. People rarely decide to book a trip at the last minute and will make a decision about where to go or stay based on their friend's experiences. For the hospitality industry, social media is more about informing guests about what is happening in the city that will help drive people to your area.

Facebook can be the most useful in this way, because posts and pages tend to spread quickly as people give you "likes." It is also free to setup a Facebook page, pretty straight forward to setup with the information involved, and affordable when wanting to advertise. Spending $50.00 on an advertising campaign can help you reach 10,000 people. That money spent also guarantees a certain amount of interaction as you are paying for the clicks on your advertisement. The best part about advertising on the site is you get to choose your target audience: age, region, and interests. It will help eliminate advertising to people that generally would not be interested in traveling or staying at vacation rentals. I generally promote the dates of my availability, and then post regularly about events that are happening in my region that people will likely want to attend.

Twitter is popular, but pales in comparison to how large and active Facebook is. The messages you send can be lost in the noise there much more easily as people tend to not listen to the businesses/brands as much as they do people they know personally or have interacted with. Twitter is again a great way to promote something in the moment, but it is far more difficult to get a message to spread there than on Facebook. The advertising is not nearly as flexible or powerful either. I would not put too much emphasis into it, personally.

NEWSLETTERS

One area that is generally overlooked when it comes to promoting a vacation rental is having a newsletter. Newsletters are easy to create and manage, and no one minds if they only receive an email once a month or less. With the right duration between emails, it can be more of a pleasant surprise and will likely be read more often than skipped over. I use a newsletter first as a mass thank you note for people that had stayed with me during the summer, and then as a reminder note for everyone that has stayed with me in the past to book again before the summer fills up.

You can create them easily using a service like Mailchimp, which is free to use until you have an extremely large audience. You can easily important the guest information for thank you notes, segment the audience so you only reach out to a certain group of your audience, and can schedule your emails so they arrive earlier in the day than you would be awake for. People can also unsubscribe at any time, which helps you avoid being labelled as a spam message.

I also provide my former guests with a discount code for the next season or match their rate again as a thank you for staying with me previously.

CRAIGSLIST AND LOCAL SITES

Craigslist is an extremely large advertising site which has its own area for vacation rental listings. It provides a lot of traffic for your listing but can be more time-consuming to manage. People tend to not read the full listings and click on the email link to ask their questions instead. They also can't see the availability on Craigslist, so making a reservation is not as quick and easy as the other portal sites.

There is a dangerous thing happening on Craigslist right now that you should be aware of. People are duplicating listings and scamming people. They will ask people to send them cash for their bookings, and then provide your number for finalizing the details on getting the keys to your place. Of course, people are rather stuck in getting their money back as it can be quite difficult to get the RCMP involved if they are dealing with small amounts of money. I tend to stick a warning on my own listing stating that people need to be aware of duplicates and that my listing is legit. Partly to give them a sense of peace when looking at my listing, but also to make them aware so they avoid other scammers. When you discover a duplicate listing, there is a bit of a process in order to get it removed. Be aware of this challenge when posting your listing on Craigslist.

Most cities now also have localized advertising portals, similar to Craigslist but not quite as big. Most should have areas to list for vacation rentals, but they likely will not be free to post on. There will be a small charge to keep the duplicates and fraudsters away. Traffic generated by these local sites will vary depending on the city. Scout out the local sites and see how many listings are active and see if they have a view count available on the listing. That will help you make the decision whether to pursue it or not.

SURVEYS

Receiving feedback from your guests is quite valuable. It informs you of areas of concern that you should be working on with your rental, or mistakes in your marketing materials. If published on a website or booking site, it informs other guests as to why they should be staying with you and what to expect. Both are extremely important in maintaining a smooth operation and attracting future guests.

With AirBnB, HomeAway, and Villas.com, the surveys are automatically sent for you. With AirBnB, the owners also get the opportunity to review their guests and inform the other hosts on the site on which guests to avoid.

For people booking directly through you, you will have to craft your own survey. It can be something simple like a few quick questions in an email, a one-page Word document, or you can build an online survey through a service like SurveyMonkey. Keep it short and simple. Anything longer than ten questions will quickly bore people and they will never fill out the entire survey. Using a service like SurveyMonkey will keep all the results in one area and tabulate the scores for you, so you can see which areas need the most improvement quickly.

CONCLUSION

Regardless of which direction you go with your marketing campaigns, there are two ultimate goals to achieve. First, you want to create interest in your property, so it gets rented in the first season and future seasons. Second, you want to create loyalty with your previous guests to encourage them to return in the following years to come. The more you create a relationship with your guests and have them return in future years, the less money you will need to spend on marketing in the future, which will make your net income that much greater.

The areas outlined should all play a role in finding and keeping your guests. Because each rental is different, you will have to find the right mix of using each area to market effectively. Doing too much marketing can push people away, but not having enough marketing will not drive people to you. Keep experimenting with the frequency and timing of your marketing to discover what works best for you. There are countless books to help you in each specific area, so keep on exploring and learning to develop your marketing skills.

LAUNCH

The timing for the launch of your vacation rental will depend on how thorough you are with each step. Researching your market area and developing a plan for marketing can be quite consuming. The main thing to keep in mind is to not rush. A poor listing profile can do more harm than good, because you may lose out on potential guests who have discovered you.

Take the time to complete each step properly and the vacation rental should be successful in its first year. The steps laid out should be completed in sequential order, but you can bounce back and forth a bit as you sketch out your ideas on how to operate your vacation rental.

When you do decide to publish your listings on the portal sites and launch your website, be patient. Do not expect your first bookings to arrive in the first few days of being live. It can take time for your first reservation to arrive. Take the time to draft up some templates in how you would like to communicate with your guests: a template for frequently asked questions, quotes, reservation confirmation details, cancellation details, and a thank you note or invitation to fill out a review after their stay. Having a template will keep your operation organized and have a consistent message, which will help you stick to your guidelines setup on the profile sites (i.e. check-in and check-out times.)

The better you are at planning and being organized, the more successful you will be in your vacation rental. Also stick to your plan as much as possible and don't let the guests guide you off the path you have developed too much. Once you start making exceptions for people, it will be harder to remember which is the exception and which is the rule. Rules are there to protect you and your property from any damage, and to keep your guests safe. Your guests will not fight too much about changing the rules, because they understand why they are in place. And if they do resist the rules, they are likely not the kind of guest you wish to have in your vacation rental.

Hopefully, this short guide has been of great interest to you and helped you make the right decision on whether to pursue being a vacation rental operator or not. It is a good jumping off point to discover the wealth of resources available at the bookstore and online to help you continue learning about the business side and greater success.

My contact information is on the next page. Feel free to reach out to me to ask any questions or seek advice.

Wishing you all the best as you join the vacation rental revolution!

APPENDIX

Vacation Rental Portals

AIRBNB

HOMEAWAY - $50.00 OFF a subscription

VILLAS.COM

ROOMORAMA - $50.00 OFF as host and/or travel

Marketing

CRAIGSLIST.ORG

SURVEYMONKEY

MAILCHIMP

WORDPRESS.COM

VACATION RENTAL THEME

Books Of Interest

How to Rent Vacation Properties by Owner

The Complete Guide to Your First Rental Property: A Step-by-Step Plan from the Experts Who Do It Every Day

Rental Property Investing for the Rest of Us: The Beginners Guide to Successful Rental Property Investing

Money Making Vacation Rentals

Essentialism - Greg McKeown

Other Sites

How to Host - blog and consultant for decorating, marketing your vacation rental

Lodgify Blog - full of tips for vacation rental property owners

FutureStay

CONTACT

James McCullough

Four Sides Hospitality Consulting

Kelownapm.com - property management in Kelowna, BC

Four Sides - personal site

Frictionless.Today

Foursides - Instagram

Email: jamesm@foursidesconsulting.com

ABOUT THE AUTHOR

James Mccullough

Having over 10 years of experience in the hospitality industry, James McCullough brings a fresh approach to property management to Sutton-Hymark Realty.

The hotel industry has trained him well in handling manager-owner and manager-tenant relationships to ensure everything is communicated effectively and in a timely manner. His role in the industry started at the front desk and grew upwards into management, eventually leading to him setting up his  own consulting firm, Four Sides Hospitality Consulting. It has helped him grow his business sense, being able to price units effectively and have success marketing the properties.

Personally, James is a single father to a young girl and has lived in Kelowna for six years now. He holds a Bachelors in Fine Arts from the University of Regina, went through the Property Management Licensing Course from Sauder School of Business at the University of British Columbia, and is fully licensed for Property Management from the Real Estate Council of British Columbia, as

of spring 2016.

www.ingramcontent.com/pod-product-compliance
Lightning Source LLC
Chambersburg PA
CBHW050317220526
45465CB00005B/2029